Fully Alive

A Family Life Education program

sponsored by
the Ontario Conference of Catholic Bishops

PEARSON
Education
Canada

Imprimatur: Richard Smith
President of the Ontario Conference of Catholic Bishops
Bishop of Pembroke, Ontario

OCCB Education Commission
Cardinal Aloysius Ambrozic
Bishop Paul-Andre Durocher (Chair)
Bishop Gerard Bergie
Bishop John Boissonneau
Bishop Robert Harris
Bishop Ronald Fabbro
Father Remi Lessard
Sister Joan Cronin

Fully Alive Advisory Committee
Mary Carr, *Algonquin Lakeshore Catholic District School Board*
Peter Crane, *Peterborough Victoria Northumberland and Clarington
    Catholic District School Board*
Moira McQueen, *Executive Director of the Canadian Catholic
    Bioethics Institute*
Ralph Peter, *Toronto Catholic District School Board*
John Podgorski, *Ottawa-Carleton Catholic District School Board*
Sandra Wilson, *executive member of the Ontario Association of
    Parents in Catholic Education*

Grade 3 Contributors
Margaret Baines, *Toronto Catholic District School Board*
Shelley MacKenzie, *London Catholic District School Boards*

General Editor: Sylvia Pegis Santin
Publisher: Patrick Gallagher
Cover Design: Sarah Orr/ArtPlus Limited
Interior Design: Sandra Sled/ArtPlus Limited

ISBN-13: 978-0-13-206937-3
ISBN-10: 0-13-206937-7

2 3 4 5 – TC – 11 10 09 08

Printed and Bound in Canada

Table of Contents

See what love the Father has given us, that we should be called children of God; and so we are.

1 John 3:1

We learn more about ourselves.
We are God's special creation.
God knows and loves each one of us.

God Knows My Name

When you were born God gave you a family. One of the first things your family did was give you your name. They chose a special name just for you.

You call the people you know by their names. The people who know you call you by your name. God also knows you, and loves you. And God knows your name.

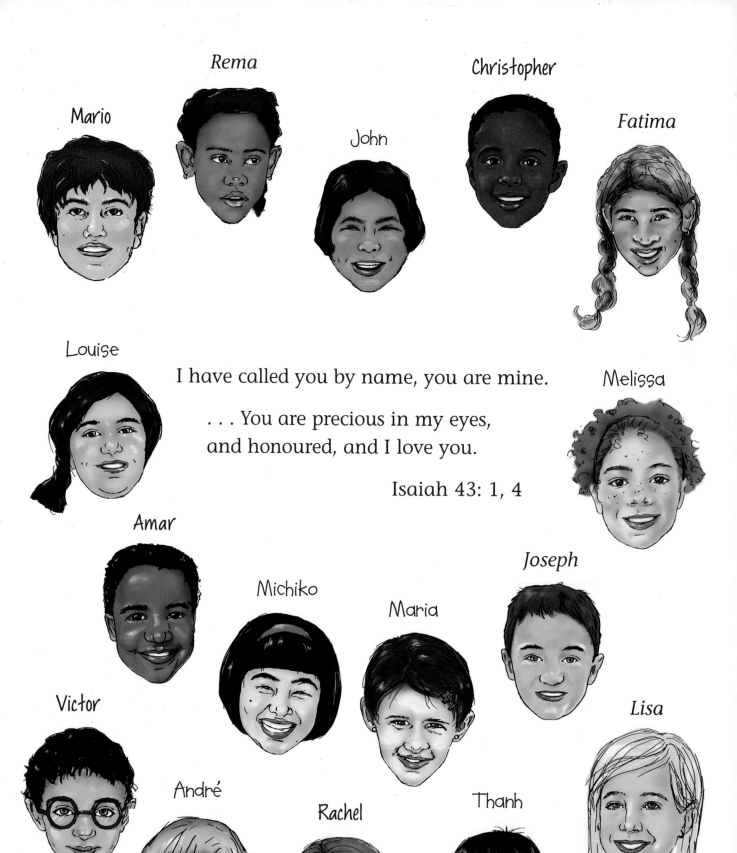

Mario

Rema

John

Christopher

Fatima

Louise

I have called you by name, you are mine.

. . . You are precious in my eyes,
and honoured, and I love you.

Isaiah 43: 1, 4

Melissa

Amar

Michiko

Maria

Joseph

Victor

André

Rachel

Thanh

Lisa

Different and Alike

Your name is special because it is part of you. But there are so many other things to know about you. Your name is just the beginning.

Here I am wearing my favourite t-shirt.

A Story About Me

Hi, I'm Eddie Petrowski. My name is really Edward, but everyone calls me Eddie. I am in Grade 3. I like reading and art, but I'm not too good at math. My mom says I'll get better if I try. I'm sort of quiet. Sometimes I'm shy. I have a big brother named Steve. He is in Grade 8. I really like drawing pictures. My dad says art is my special talent. Steve's special talent is sports. You should see him play hockey.

The End

Eddie is a unique person. That means there isn't anyone else just like him.

Eddie has a special talent for art. There are some things he likes and some things he doesn't like. Usually he's quiet and sometimes he's shy. That's his special personality. He is happy to be Eddie Petrowski.

You have your own special talents. You have likes and dislikes. There are some things you find easy to learn and some things you find difficult.

You have your own special personality. Maybe you are quiet and shy like Eddie. Or maybe you love to talk and meet new people. What's your special way of being a person?

Whatever it is, God knows and loves you as the unique person you are.

Some Unique People

only child

serious

very tall

dislikes going to bed

likes computer games

out-going

lots of freckles

oldest child

likes baseball

dislikes loud thunder

friendly smile

middle child

quick-tempered

likes writing stories

dislikes peanut butter

energetic

blue eyes

youngest child

likes bike-riding

dislikes sitting still

God made each one of us unique. We enjoy our differences. It would be very boring if we were all the same.

But God also made us alike in many ways. This helps us understand each other because we share so much. We can all think and choose. We share many feelings. We all need other people. We need our families and our friends, and they need us. We can't get along without each other.

Different and the same. That's the way God made us.

You and Me

There are all kinds of people,
And one of them's me.
Just one special person
Whom God likes to see.

There are all kinds of people,
And one of them's you.
One more special person,
With me, that makes two.

There are all kinds of people,
Whom God likes to see.
Each one is special,
Like you and like me.

All Kinds of Feelings

What do you do when you're happy? Do you smile and laugh? Do you jump up and down and make lots of noise? What happens when you're sad? Do you cry really hard or do you curl up and hide your face. What about when you're angry? Do you get very quiet or do you explode like a rocket?

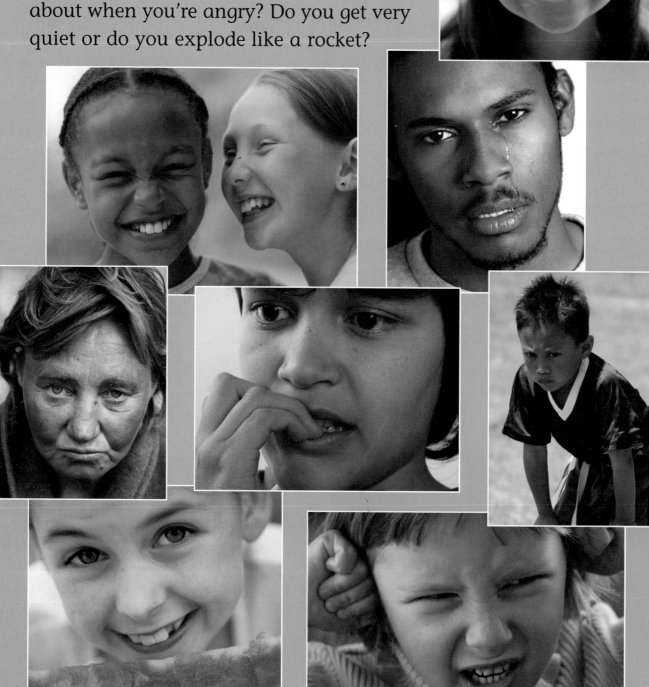

Everyone has feelings. We all feel happy sometimes, sad sometimes, and angry sometimes. But we don't all show our feelings in the same way.

Remember Eddie Petrowski? Eddie's best friend is John. John gets angry very easily. His face gets all red. He wants to hit something. Eddie doesn't get angry very often. But when he does, he gets very quiet and wants to be by himself.

Here is another difference between Eddie and John. On the first day of school, Eddie always gets nervous, and his stomach feels sick. But John never feels nervous. He feels excited and happy.

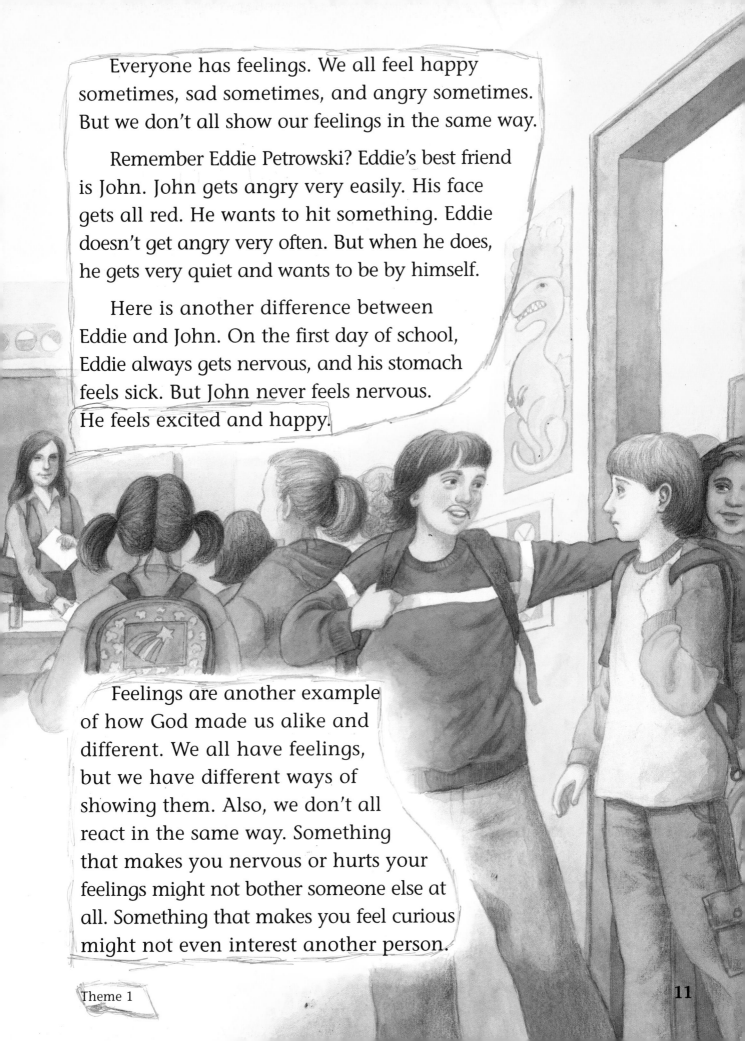

Feelings are another example of how God made us alike and different. We all have feelings, but we have different ways of showing them. Also, we don't all react in the same way. Something that makes you nervous or hurts your feelings might not bother someone else at all. Something that makes you feel curious might not even interest another person.

All the different people in your class make it an exciting place to be. But things don't always go that well. Sometimes there are conflicts. That's when it's important to think about what we do with our feelings.

• • •

One day, Eddie came home from school very upset. He went to his room and sat on his bed. He was thinking about what had happened.

Eddie and John were playing together during recess. Adam, who was in their class, started teasing Eddie, and calling him names. When Eddie ignored him, Adam pushed Eddie and almost knocked him over. That's when John got very angry, and hit Adam. Now John was in trouble, and Eddie felt as if it were his fault.

After dinner, Eddie finally told his parents what had happened. They were sorry he was so upset, and his dad explained to him that it was not his fault. John was trying to be a good friend, but he shouldn't have hit Adam. They talked for a while, and Eddie felt better by the time he went to bed.

. . .

We can't choose how we feel, but we can choose how we act. When we are in charge of our feelings, we stop and think about the way God wants us to treat other people. But if our feelings are in charge of us, we often do something we are sorry for later. We choose to do something we know is wrong, which is a sin. When this happens, we need to ask God for forgiveness and try to make up for any harm we have done.

Theme 1

We Share Our Talents and Gifts

Eddie was so proud. His brother Steve had scored the winning goal of the hockey game. Everyone was cheering.

Eddie's dad put his arm around Eddie. "Great game, wasn't it?" his dad said.

"Was it ever!" Eddie said. "I wish I could play like that."

"And score goals?" his dad asked.

Eddie nodded.

They walked toward the dressing room to meet Steve.

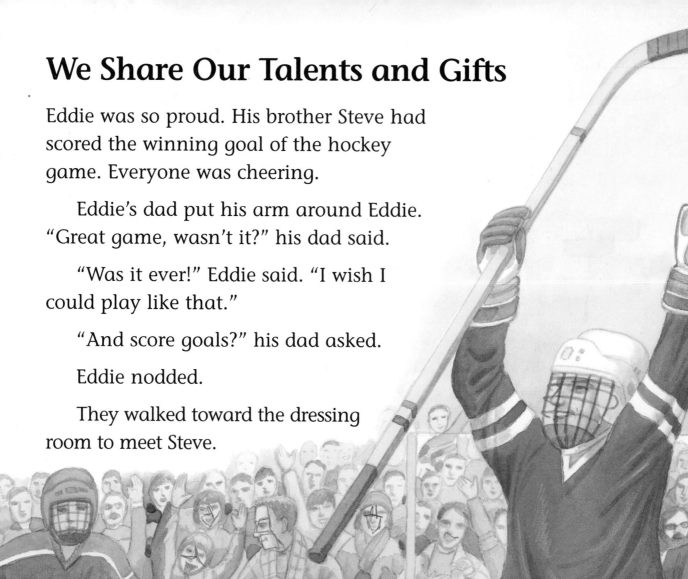

"You know what?" Eddie's father said. "When I was your age I wanted to be good at sports too. But I wasn't. I was good at making things and fixing things, but not at sports."

"How come?" Eddie asked.

"That's just the way it is. We have different talents."

"And Steve's is sports?" Eddie said.

"Yes, that's one of his talents. And you have a special talent for art."

"I helped Steve with the cover of his project," Eddie said proudly.

"I know you did. You share your talent with Steve, and he shares his talent with you."

"How does he share his with me," Eddie asked. He looked puzzled.

"Did you have fun today?" his dad asked.

"Sure" Eddie said.

Steve came out of the dressing room.

"Hey, Steve! Great goal!" Eddie shouted, and he ran toward his brother.

• • •

God gave each person special talents. Some people are good at sports, like Steve. Some are good at art, like Eddie. Some people can tell stories or make music. What are your special talents?

God also gave us other gifts that we all share. We can all be generous and thoughtful. It doesn't take a special talent to be kind and patient. But we do have to try hard and ask God to help us.

God wants us to develop our talents and gifts, and share them with others. When we share our gifts and talents, we are sharing ourselves. We are helping to make the world a good place to be.

Mei Lin

Quiet, friendly
Listening, smiling, helping,
Like a sturdy rock,
The artist.

Henri

Funny, clever,
Joking, talking, laughing,
As cheerful as a big smile,
The entertainer.

Barbara

Busy, chatty,
Jumping, climbing, running,
As fast as the wind,
My best friend.

Christopher

Serious, kind,
Practising, thinking, imagining,
Like a quiet song,
The music maker.

My soul takes pleasure in three things; agreement among members of a family, friendship between neighbours, and a wife and husband who live in harmony.

Cf. Sirach 25:1

We learn about some of the important people in our lives. Our family members and friends help us to be loving people.

Our Families

How do you write your name on your work at school? Eddie Petrowski always writes his name like this:

Eddie P.

He thinks it takes too long to write Petrowski. Maybe you have a long last name like Eddie. Or do you have a short last name like Smith or Chan or Bruno?

Your last name is your family name. It tells people something very important about you — you belong to a family.

Families are made up of parents and children, but that's not all. There are also grandparents, aunts, uncles, and cousins. They are part of your extended family. Extended family means your big family.

Did you ever ask about your family name? Eddie asked his mom. She told him that Petrowski means "son of Peter." It's a Polish name. Mrs. Petrowski's family name is Lafleur. It's a French name that means "the flower."

If your family comes from Korea, your name might be Kim. Kim means "gold." Maybe you have an Irish name like Murphy. Murphy means someone who is related to Murchadh. He was a famous sea fighter. Or maybe your family name is Martello. That's an Italian name that means "hammer."

Do you know what your family name means?

Petrowski

Lafleur

Kim

Martello

Murphy

People are unique, and families are too. Each family has its own special way of being a family. Each family has special customs.

- The Petrowskis always spends Easter with Mr. Petrowski's mother. She lives in southern Ontario, and it's a long car ride from their home. Eddie and Steve look forward to seeing Babcia, which means Grandma in Polish. They especially like to watch her colour Easter eggs. She creates tiny criss-cross patterns and flowers, deer, hens, and suns on the eggs. She learned how to do this from her grandmother. It wouldn't be Easter without Babcia's coloured eggs.

- Eddie's mother has a custom from her family that has become part of the Petrowski family. During the winter when she was a girl, the Lafleur family went to Sunday mass, and then went skating on a nearby pond. The Petrowski family also goes skating after church, but not on a pond. Each winter Mr. Petrowski floods the backyard and turns it into a rink. Sometimes the neighbours join in, and everyone has a great time. It wouldn't be winter without a backyard skating rink.

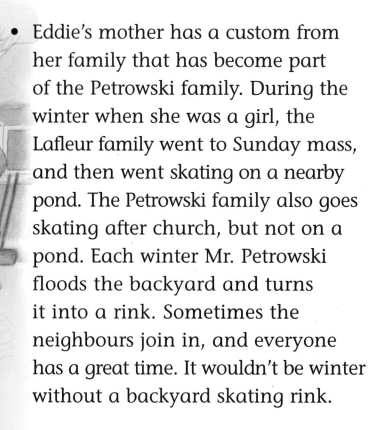

Your family may be big or it may be small. Your grandparents, aunts, uncles and cousins might live near you or far away. There might be six people in your family or just two. But it's your special family, and it's an important part of who you are.

Each family has its own way of being a family. Family customs are part of that unique way. Easter eggs and skating on a Sunday afternoon are just two of Eddie's favourite family customs. What are your favourite family customs?

Family Love is Open

It was the day before Christmas, and everyone in the Petrowski family was very busy. They were getting ready for a family Christmas Eve dinner.

Before long, the house was full. There were Mrs. Petrowski's parents, Grand-mère and Grand-père, two uncles, three aunts, and three cousins. Then Angela and her husband, Richard, arrived. Angela worked with Eddie's Aunt Louise. Richard and Angela were so happy to be part of a family on Christmas Eve. Their own families lived very far away.

After a wonderful dinner, it was soon time for Christmas Eve mass. The front hall of the house was quite crowded as everyone tried to find the right boots and coats. Mr. Petrowski and Richard had a little mix-up with their hats that made everyone laugh.

The church looked beautiful, and it was full of people. There was a Christmas crèche at the front. Eddie's teacher had told the class that Christmas was a very special family celebration, not just for them, but also for Jesus, Mary, and Joseph.

After church, the Petrowski family said goodbye to all their relatives and to Richard and Angela. Everyone said Joyeux Noël, and there were lots of hugs. It had been a wonderful Christmas Eve celebration.

When they finally got home, Steve and Eddie could hardly wait to open one of their presents. That was another family custom — one present each on Christmas Eve, but the rest had to wait until morning. When Eddie opened his present, he was very surprised. His father had made an artist's box for him, and filled it with paints and brushes.

• • •

Family love is like a door that is always open. It says, "Welcome. Come in. We belong together." This is what God says to each one of us. When family love is open to others, it helps us understand God's love.

When family members and special friends can't be with us, we can still share our love. We visit them. We talk on the telephone. We e-mail or write letters. With the Internet, we can send instant messages and talk to each other face-to-face.

But the most important way we share our love is through prayer. Jesus grew up in a family, and he knows how precious our families are. We ask Jesus to watch over the people we love.

Family Changes

When Shane Carson was five years old, his father's mother came to live with them. It was a big change for her, and for the family. But before long, they couldn't imagine their life without her. And she couldn't imagine not being able to see her grandchildren — Shane, Beth, Pamela, and Donna — every day.

All of the Carson children play soccer and their grandmother was their biggest fan. She often came to the park to watch them play, and she cheered louder than anyone else. Shane's oldest sister, Pamela, thought it was a little embarrassing, but Shane loved it.

Shane also loved playing tricks on his grandmother because they made her laugh so hard. Once he put a rubber toad on her bed. When his mom scolded him, his grandmother said, "Don't be cross with him. That's the most fun I've had all day!"

The next day, Shane opened his lunch at school and there was the toad!

Last summer, just after Shane turned eight, his grandmother died. Everyone in the family was very sad. Their home seemed so strange without her.

One day, as Shane walked home from school, he was feeling really sad. His grandmother had always been there when he got home. It just wasn't the same without her. "It's not fair," he muttered to himself.

Later that day, Shane talked to his dad about how he felt. "Maybe if she hadn't lived with us, I wouldn't miss her so much," he said.

"That might be true," his dad said, "but think of what you would have missed. You have so many good memories. All the fun and laughter you shared is part of you forever. She loved you so much."

Shane thought about what his dad was saying.

"You know, Shane," his dad explained. "People don't stop loving us after they die. And we don't stop loving them. You're here and your grandma's with God. But the loving doesn't end."

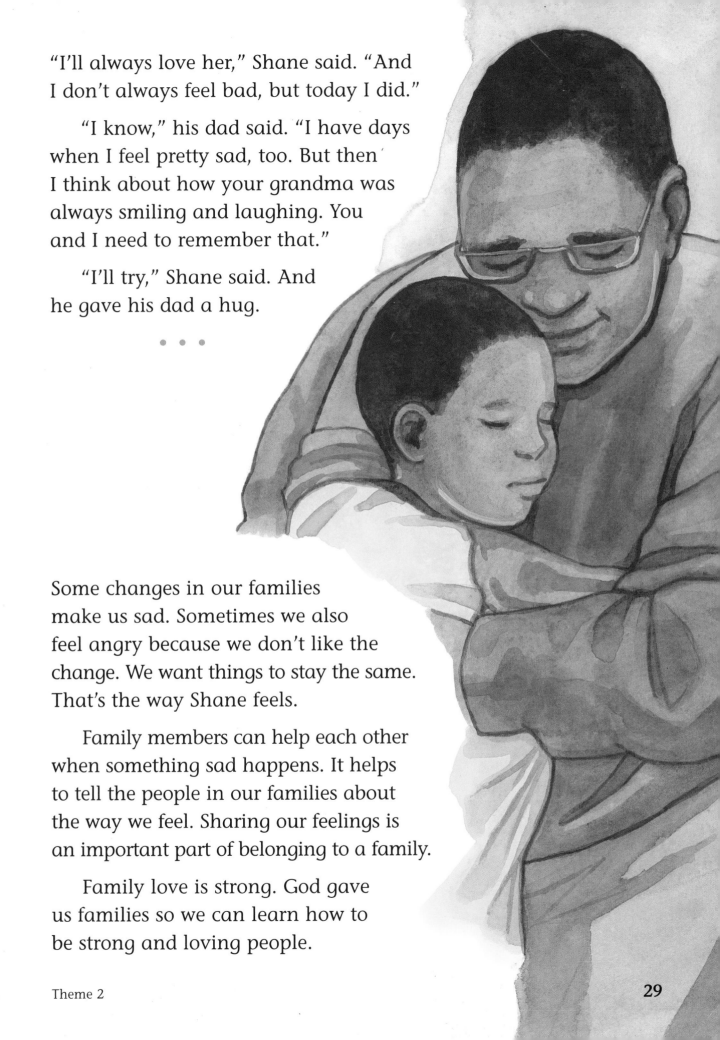

"I'll always love her," Shane said. "And I don't always feel bad, but today I did."

"I know," his dad said. "I have days when I feel pretty sad, too. But then I think about how your grandma was always smiling and laughing. You and I need to remember that."

"I'll try," Shane said. And he gave his dad a hug.

• • •

Some changes in our families make us sad. Sometimes we also feel angry because we don't like the change. We want things to stay the same. That's the way Shane feels.

Family members can help each other when something sad happens. It helps to tell the people in our families about the way we feel. Sharing our feelings is an important part of belonging to a family.

Family love is strong. God gave us families so we can learn how to be strong and loving people.

Memories of Grandma

Sisters and Brothers

There are four children in the Carson family.

Hi, I'm Pamela and I'm eleven. I'm the oldest. That means I get to stay up later than my sisters and brother. Also my mom and dad depend on me a lot. I always have to look after the other kids, especially Donna. And when we argue, guess who gets blamed? Other than that, I like being the oldest.

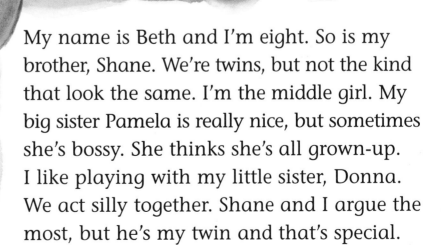

My name is Beth and I'm eight. So is my brother, Shane. We're twins, but not the kind that look the same. I'm the middle girl. My big sister Pamela is really nice, but sometimes she's bossy. She thinks she's all grown-up. I like playing with my little sister, Donna. We act silly together. Shane and I argue the most, but he's my twin and that's special.

I'm Shane and I'm the only boy. That makes me like an only child. I get to have my own room, even if it is really small. My three sisters have to share a room. They say it's not fair. My sister Pamela is bossy, but she's okay. Beth and I wrestle on Pamela's bed and she gets mad at us. Donna's the littlest and she's funny. She tells silly jokes.

I'm Donna, and the youngest. I'm five and a half. I tell funny jokes and everyone laughs. I like playing with my sisters and brother. But sometimes they do things together and they don't want me around. You should hear how loud I yell at them! But I'm trying not to because mom says it's not very nice.

Are you a brother or a sister? Are you an only child? Are you the oldest, middle, or youngest child? Everyone has a special place in the family. There are some good things about your special place and some not so good things.

Sometimes you might wish that you could trade places with someone else. But you know that you can't. So it's important to learn how to be the best sister or brother or only child you can be.

It would be nice to have someone to play with all the time.

I'm always too little and everyone tells me what to do.

Sometimes people expect too much of me. I didn't ask to be the oldest!

I get left out sometimes because I'm not the oldest or the youngest.

Being a sister or a brother is a special kind of friendship. You might not always think so, especially when you don't get along.

But you belong to the same family. You spend a lot of time together. You play and work together, and you learn from each other. You learn to share and to compromise. Compromise means settling an argument fairly. When you compromise everyone gives in a little. Then you can find a solution to the problem.

Learning to get along with others is something everyone needs to do. Having a sister or a brother is an important way of learning how.

What is a Friend?

A friend is someone you always look forward to seeing. Friends enjoy each other. It's fun to be with a friend.

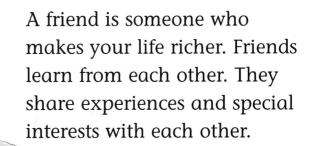

A friend is someone who makes your life richer. Friends learn from each other. They share experiences and special interests with each other.

A friend is someone you care about. Friends try to help each other. They comfort each other when things go wrong.

Beth has a good friend named Christine. Christine stays with the Carsons after school until her mother comes home from work. They have a lot of fun together, but sometimes they disagree. This is what they sound like:

"It's my turn to go first."

"It is not. It's my turn. You always try to go first."

"I do not! You're cheating!"

"I don't want to go out. I want to play games on the computer."

"Well, I don't! I want to go out to the playground."

"Well, I'm not going."

"You're mean."

Beth and Christine need to learn how to settle their arguments without fighting. They need to learn to compromise. Both of them have to give in a little.

Sometimes they need some help. Beth's mother helped them solve the problem of who goes first. She suggested that they write down who went first. Beth and Christine liked that solution. It was a good compromise.

God made us to be with other people
and to have friends. No matter how
old we are, that never changes.

Friends

What belongs together
Like running shoes and feet,
Or mustard with a hot dog,
Or blankets and a sheet?

What belongs together
Like crackers go with cheese,
Or birthday cake with ice cream,
Or thank-you and a please?

What belongs together
Like hamburgers and fries,
Or jelly in a sandwich,
Or winning and a prize?

Friends belong together
Like sticky goes with glue,
Or sniffles with a head cold,
Or laces and a shoe.

Being Part of the Group

How will these stories end?

The Baseball Player

Zach is not a very good baseball player. When his classmates choose teams, he's usually picked last. Some of his friends are having an after-school game. Zach asks them, "Hey, can I play, too?" What do they say?

Meili and Lucy

Meili and Lucy are good friends. This year there is a new girl named Kim in their class. After school one day, Meili and Lucy are walking home together. Kim runs up to them and says, "Meili, would you like to come to my house to play?" What happens next?

A New Club

Nicky, Kyle, and John are starting a club. They are very excited about it. Angelo comes up to them and asks, "What are you doing?" "We're planning our club," they answer. "Can I be in your club?" Angelo asks. What do they say?

Have you ever shared a treat with your friends? Imagine that you have four pieces of candy. You can give one each to three friends and have one for yourself.

Being friendly is also something we can share. But it's not like candy. You can't use it up. You have enough friendliness to share with everyone. In fact, the more you share it, the more you have.

Friendliness is like family love. It welcomes everyone. When we're friendly we try to find a way to include people. We all want to be included. When we're left out of the group, we don't feel very happy. No one wants to be excluded.

Is your classroom a friendly place? Can you think of ways to make it friendlier?

3

. . . God created humankind in his image . . . male and female he created them.

Genesis 1:27

We learn more about mothers and fathers
and God's plan for new human life.
Some of us are males. Some of us are females.
That is the way God created us.
We also learn more about the way
we grow and change after we are born.

Special Events

Mr. and Mrs. Carson have been away for the weekend. There were celebrating their wedding anniversary. The children were very glad when their mom and dad came back. They all talked at the same time.

"Did you bring me anything."
"Did you have a good time?"
"Will you take us next time?"
"Are you going again next year?"
"We really missed you."

Their dad answered all their questions at once. "Yes, yes, maybe, and I don't know. And we really missed you, too."

"We sure did," Mrs. Carson said, and she gave them each another hug.

• • •

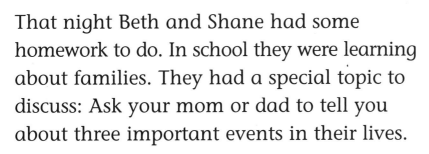

That night Beth and Shane had some homework to do. In school they were learning about families. They had a special topic to discuss: Ask your mom or dad to tell you about three important events in their lives.

"Shane and I figured out one important event," Beth said to her mother. "Your anniversary."

"That is a big event," her mom said. "But we wouldn't have an anniversary unless we got married. So that's my first event. My second is when all of you were born. And my third is when we moved from Barbados to Canada. You were just a baby, Pamela."

"What about you, Dad?" Shane asked.

"Well, mine are the same as your mother's," he said. "I remember that day we arrived in Canada. It was so cold! But I have a fourth important event to add to the list. I'll bet you no one in your class will have this event."

"What is it?" Shane asked.

"It's something that happens every night. Suddenly, it gets nice and quiet around here. Can you guess why?" his dad teased.

"I know," Beth shouted. "It's because we're all asleep!"

"Oh, Dad," Shane said.

There are many important events for families. Did you know that when you celebrate your birthday, it's an anniversary celebration? It's the anniversary of the day you were born.

The day people get married is another important event. There is a special celebration in the church for the sacrament of marriage.

When a man and woman decide to get married, they have made a very important decision. They love each other very much. They want to spend their whole lives together. They ask God to bless them and to help them have a good marriage.

A husband and wife begin a new life together. With God's help, their love grows stronger. They want to share their special love. They do this is by becoming parents. It is a very happy time for a husband and wife when children arrive.

Your life began because of the special love of your parents and because of God's love. God wanted you to be here. Nothing can ever change that.

Beginning Life

The next day at dinner, Mr. Carson asked Beth and Shane, "Did you talk about the three important events in class?"

"We did, and a lot of people said getting married and having children, the same as you and Mom," Shane said.

"I'm not surprised," his dad said. "Getting married and having children is great."

"Michael's mom told him the most important event was when he was adopted," Beth said. "She said that the night before he was going to arrive, she and his dad couldn't sleep. They were so excited that they were awake most of the night."

"What's adopted?" Donna asked.

"You know how babies grow inside their mothers?" Mrs. Carson said.

Donna nodded.

"Well, sometimes a mom and dad can't look after a baby. But they want the baby to have a good home. So they let another mother and father adopt the baby."

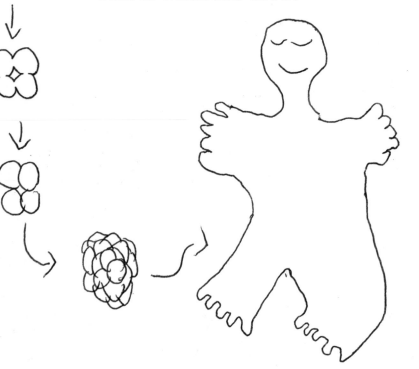

"Am I adopted?" Donna asked.

"No, you grew inside Mom," Pamela said. "You started from a tiny cell, right Mom?"

"That's right."

"Then how did she get bigger, like a baby?" Shane asked.

"Here, I'll show you on this piece of paper," Pamela said.

This is what she drew.

"That's a good drawing," Mrs. Carson said. "There's a special word for when that one cell begins — conception."

"What does that mean?" Beth asked.

"Well, it's the very moment when a tiny part from the mother and a tiny part from the father join together and become one cell," her mother explained.

Theme 3

"We learned about conception at school," Pamela said. "And there's all sorts of information in that one little cell. The colour of your eyes and hair, if you're going to be tall or short, if you look more like your mom or more like your dad."

"That's true," her mom said. "Now, let's get this table cleared."

"I want to talk some more about before babies are born," Beth said.

"We will," her mother said, "tomorrow."

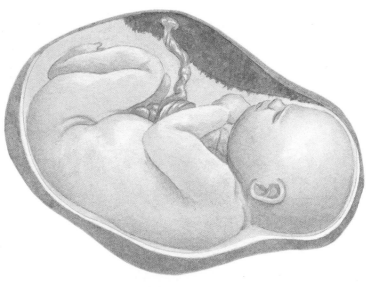

The cell that begins each person's life comes from a tiny part from the father, called a sperm, and a tiny part from the mother, called an ovum. The sperm and the ovum join together inside the mother and become one cell. At this moment of conception something wonderful and sacred has happened. A new human life has begun. It comes from God and from the mother and the father.

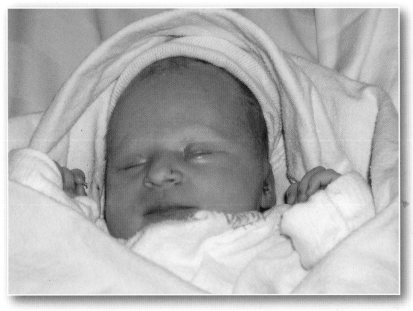

From a tiny cell . . . to a new baby.

Our First Home

The next day Mrs. Carson showed Beth and Shane a book about babies before they are born.

"See," she said, "here's the cell dividing, like the picture Pamela drew. And look at this picture. Now it looks like a baby."

"Doesn't the baby get too big to fit inside the mother?" Beth asked.

"There's lots of room," her mother said. "You know, you and Shane grew inside of me at the same time, and there was plenty of room. The uterus just stretches and stretches as the baby gets bigger. That's the way God made women."

"How does the baby eat?" Shane asked.

"Let's look at another picture," his mother said. "And then I can show you."

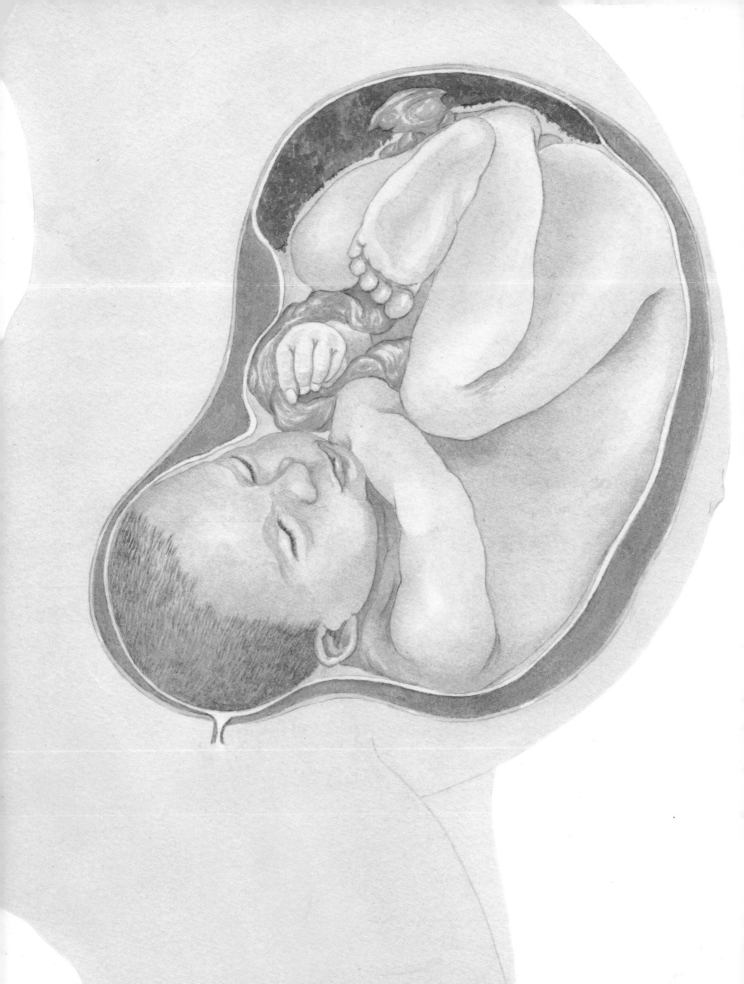

"Do you see how the baby is attached to the mother by a cord? It's called the umbilical cord," Mrs. Carson explained. "The baby's food comes from the mother's body, through the umbilical cord to the baby."

Beth looked at the picture. "How does the baby go to the bathroom?" she asked.

"The same way," her mom said. "The waste from the baby's body goes through the umbilical cord and into the mother's body."

"And then it comes out of her body when she goes to the bathroom?" Beth asked.

"Yes, that's right," her mom said.

"How does the baby breathe?" Shane asked.

"Well, the baby gets oxygen through the cord. Babies can't begin to breathe the way you do until after they are born."

Beth and Shane looked at the picture. Then Shane said, "I think the baby has a very good home."

• • •

Shane is right. The uterus is a very good home for the baby.

Beth and Shane are learning a lot about what happens before we are born. They learned more about the uterus and the umbilical cord. That's the baby's special life support system, just like an astronaut's. Everything the baby needs comes through the umbilical cord.

The mother's uterus is a very safe home for her baby. The baby is inside a special sac filled with fluid that looks like water. The baby floats in the fluid and is protected from bumps. The baby lives in this warm, safe home for about nine months. And the mother and father wait to meet this new little person.

Welcoming the New Baby

Beth and Shane had lots of questions
as they looked at the book.

"How does the mother know when the
baby's ready to come out?" Beth asked.

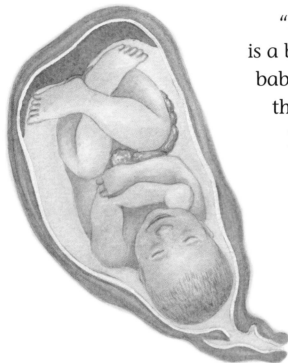

"Look at this picture. The uterus
is a big muscle and it can push on the
baby," Mrs. Carson explained. "When
the mother starts to feel the uterus
pushing, she knows that it's time
for the baby to be born. Then
she and the father go to the
hospital. Or she might have
the baby at home."

"Then what happens?"
Shane asked.

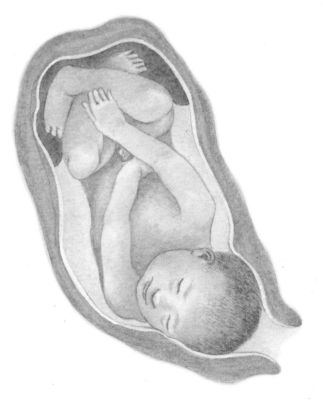

"Well, the uterus keeps
pushing and the bottom of it
opens. Then the baby's head
can fit through the opening."

"And then the baby comes
out through here," said Beth,
pointing at the picture.

"Yes, through the mother's
vagina. It's also called the birth
canal because the baby moves
through it to be born," her
mom explained.

"Oh look," Mrs. Carson said, and she pointed at a picture. "A brand new baby, just born!"

"It's so little," Shane said. "Was I that little?"

"I think it's cute," Beth said.

• • •

The mother and father are so happy to meet their new baby. Sometimes the mother feeds her baby right away from her breast. In a little while she will have lots of milk and she can breastfeed her baby whenever it's hungry. Some mothers feed their babies from a bottle. All babies need milk after they are born so that they can grow big and strong.

Babies also need lots of love. They need people to hold them, talk to them, and sing to them. They need a special family to say, "Welcome to the world! We are so happy God sent you to us."

Hush Little Baby

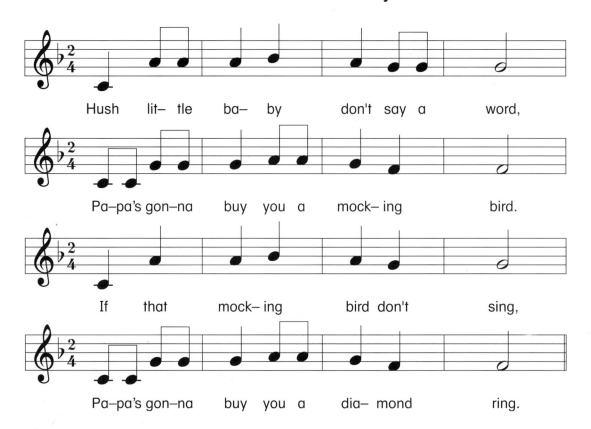

Hush lit—tle ba—by don't say a word,

Pa—pa's gon—na buy you a mock—ing bird.

If that mock—ing bird don't sing,

Pa—pa's gon—na buy you a dia—mond ring.

And if that diamond ring turns brass,
Papa's going to buy you a looking glass.

And if that looking glass gets broke,
Papa's going to buy you a billy goat.

And if that billy goat won't pull,
Papa's going to buy you a cart and bull.

And if that cart and bull turn over,
Papa's going to buy you a dog named Rover.

And if that dog named Rover won't bark,
Papa's going to buy you a horse and cart.

And if that horse and cart fall down,
You'll still be the sweetest little baby in town.

58

Beth and Shane were still looking at the picture of the newborn baby.

"I wonder if it's a boy or a girl," Beth said.

"That's the first question most people ask," her mom said. "Is it a girl or a boy?"

"Well, when we were born, you got both!" Shane said.

His mother smiled. "Wasn't I lucky," she said. "But you know, it really doesn't matter. Girls are wonderful and so are boys."

"I'd rather be a girl," Beth said.

"And I'd rather be a boy," said Shane.

"And I'm glad you're both happy!" their mother said, laughing.

• • •

We Grow and Change

New babies seem very small and helpless. But they don't stay that way for long! You don't remember, but you were very busy during the first year of your life.

Age	In one year, most babies begin to:			
0 – 3 months	• enjoy looking at faces	• smile at people	• play with their hands	• lift their heads when on their stomachs
3 – 6 months	• roll over	• reach for objects	• shake a rattle to hear the noise	• eat some solid food
6 – 9 months	• sit without help	• crawl on their bellies	• enjoy peek-a-boo	• tell strangers from people they know
9 – 12 months	• crawl on their hands and knees	• walk with help	• stand up without help	• say their first word

You were also very busy growing. At the end of their first year, most babies weigh three times as much as they did when they were born, and are about half again as tall. Can you imagine how big you would be now if you had kept on growing at that rate?

By the time you were three, you would be about the size of a large man!

By the time you were six, you would be as tall as a full-grown giraffe!

But you didn't keep growing that quickly. You started to slow down after your first birthday.

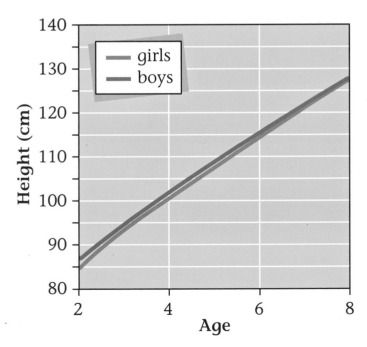

This graph shows you the average height for girls and boys when they are two, four, six, and eight years old.

Where do you fit?

Here are a few more changes since you were born:

- Teeth — By the time you were a year old, you probably had six or eight teeth, Those first baby teeth are also the first ones you lose to make room for your permanent teeth.

- Feet — You had chubby little feet when you were a baby. How big are your feet now?

- Physical skills — Most babies begin to walk without help when they are about one year old. Just think what you have learned to do since then — hop, run, jump, skip, go up and down stairs, kick a ball, balance on one foot, and so much more.

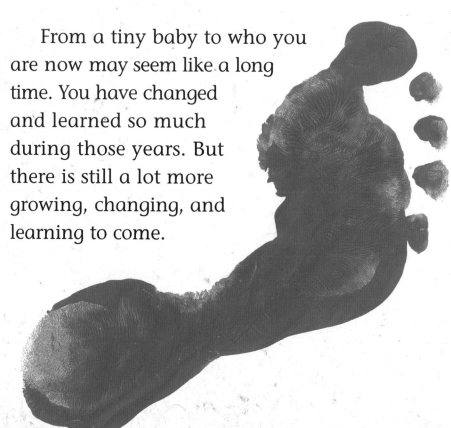

From a tiny baby to who you are now may seem like a long time. You have changed and learned so much during those years. But there is still a lot more growing, changing, and learning to come.

4

. . . let your yes be yes and your no be no . . .

James 5:12

We learn about commitments and decisions. We ask God and other people to help us keep our commitments and to make good decisions.

Families Have Commitments

Sometimes families are very busy!
Does your family calendar look like this?

Eddie is very excited. Today he found out that his project was going to be in the school science fair next Tuesday night. Only three projects were chosen from each class. Eddie's was a model of a volcano.

That night Eddie told everyone his big news.

"That's great!" his dad said.

"When is the science fair?" his mom asked.

"Next Tuesday. After dinner, from 7 to 9."

His mother's face fell. "I can't go," she said. "That's my class night, and I have a test."

"And I have to work late all next week," his dad said. "What can we do?"

Eddie looked very upset. "It's not fair," he said. "I really want you to come." Then he went upstairs to his room.

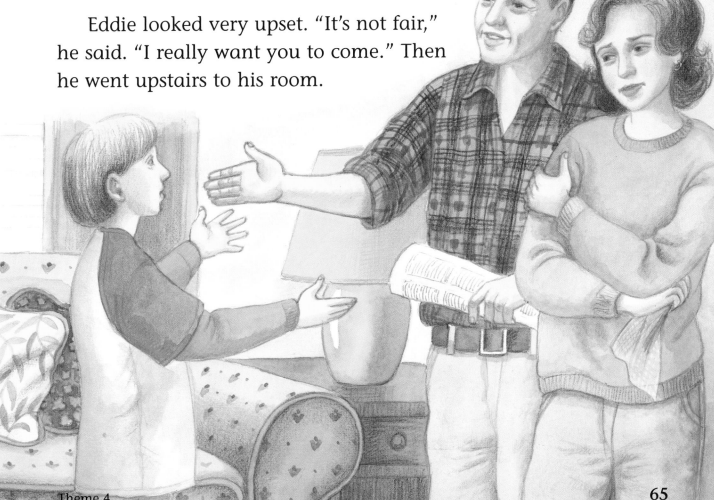

Later that evening, Eddie had a talk with his dad.

"Your mom really wants to go, Eddie. But she can't miss her test. You know how hard she's studied. I want to go, too, but I have to work."

"I know," Eddie said, "but I want you both to be there."

"We'll work something out," his dad said.

By the next morning, Eddie's mom and dad had come up with solution.

"Steve will go with you and take pictures of the science fair for us," his mom explained.

"I will?" Steve said.

"Yes, you will. I don't think Eddie has missed one of your hockey games," she reminded him.

"I'll go, Mom," Steve said, "I was just kidding."

"It's a good plan, Dad," Eddie said.

• • •

VOLCANO

METHOD

Being a member of a family means having commitments. A commitment is a responsibility that you try very hard to live up to.

Family members have very important commitments to each other. Because they care about each other, they make sure they spend time together. When there's a disagreement, they try hard to settle it. When there are jobs to be done around the house, everyone helps.

Family members also have commitments outside the family — working, helping at the parish, going to school, or playing on a team.

God wants us to become loving people who try hard to keep our family commitments. That's what Eddie's family did. His mom and dad found a way to show Eddie they cared about him and were proud of him.

It's not always easy to be a good family member. We need lots of help from each other and from God.

Learning About Decisions

In Eddie's neighbourhood soccer teams play once a week when the weather gets warm. Eddie's friend John played last year and said it was a lot of fun. Mr. Petrowski took Eddie to the community centre to register.

REGISTER FOR SOCCER

"We're glad to have you sign up," said the woman who took Eddie's form. Then she asked Mr. Petrowski, "Would you like to coach? All our coaches are parents and we could used a few more."

"That would be great!" Eddie exclaimed.

"I'm not sure," Eddie's dad said to the woman. "Can I let you know?"

"Sure," she answered.

"Why don't you want to be a coach, Dad?" Eddie asked on the way home.

"I didn't say I didn't want to. But I have to think about it."

"It would really be fun," Eddie said.

"It would be fun because we could do it together," his dad agreed. "But I have a lot of commitments already. And I really don't know anything about coaching."

"You'd be good at it, Dad."

"I'm not as sure about that as you are," his dad said. "And I want to talk to your mother about it. Then I'll make a decision."

"Well, I think you should," Eddie said.

"I know what you think," his dad laughed. "But I have to do my own thinking."

• • •

Decisions! Decisions! Everyone has to learn
how to make good ones.

We Get Help With Our Decisions

The school year is almost over. In a few weeks Eddie is going to a special one-week art program at the community centre. He wanted to go last year, but he wasn't old enough.

On Saturday morning the telephone rang and Eddie answered it. It was John's mother. She asked to speak to Eddie's mom.

"John's parents have rented a cottage for a week," his mom said when she got off the phone. "They're inviting you to go with them."

"Can I, Mom? Can I? Please!" Eddie asked.

"Hold on a minute. Your dad and I need to talk about it, but there's a problem, Eddie. It's the same week as your art program."

"Oh, no!" Eddie cried.

Eddie's mom and dad decided that if he wanted to, Eddie could go to John's cottage. They also checked with the community centre, but the other art program was full.

"I don't know what to do, Mom," Eddie said. "I want to go to the cottage and the art program."

"I know," his mom said. "Maybe I can help you make up your mind." She gave him a piece of paper, and asked him to write the words COTTAGE and ART CAMP at the top, and then draw a line down the middle between them.

"Now," she said. "Let's talk about each choice. You know they would both be fun, so you can write that under each one."

Eddie and his mom talked for a while. She asked him some questions he hadn't thought about, like:

"Which do you enjoy more — swimming and fishing or drawing and painting?"

"Could you do the art program or go to the cottage next summer?"

"How do you feel about being away from home for a week?"

Eddie decided to finish the list in his bedroom. He had a lot to think about. His brother Steve came in and looked at Eddie's list. He thought Eddie should go to the cottage, but Steve didn't enjoy art.

Finally, Eddie finished his list. "Mom," he shouted, "I've made a decision!"

Some decisions are easy to make, and some are difficult. Sometimes you have to decide between two good things. That's the kind of decision Eddie had to make.

Sometimes you have to decide between something that is right and something that is wrong. You want to go to the park after school with your friends. But you're supposed to go straight home. What will you do?

Everyone has to learn how to make good decisions. Our parents and teachers can help us. Eddie's mom didn't make a decision for him, but she helped him figure out what he needed to think about.

Sometimes Eddie makes bad decisions. He disobeys his parents and they're not very happy with him. They might decide to punish him, but they always try to talk to him about what happened. They want to help him grow up to be a good person.

Are you wondering what Eddie decided? Look at this list. What do you think he chose?

Art Camp	Cottage
1. Fun	1. Fun
2. At Home	2. Away from home
3. I can go next year.	3. I don't know if I can go next year
4. I don't know anyone at art camp.	4. John is my best friend.
5. I love art.	5. Swimming is O.K.

5

The heavens are yours,
and the earth also is yours;
The world and all that is in it,
you have founded them.

Psalm 89:11

We learn more about the people
who live and work in the world.
We depend on each other's work.
We try to work hard and do
the best job we can.

The World is Full of Wonderful People

There are so many people in the world! They live as close to you as next door and as far away as the other side of the world. And God made each one of them.

Some of them live very differently from you. Some families live in the desert. Some families live on water, on a boat. Do you think you would enjoy living on a boat?

All over the world people have their own ways of living, too. Some of these ways are quite different from yours. Think of the many different foods people eat, the languages they speak, and the clothes they wear. All of these differences make the world an interesting and exciting place.

But we are also alike in many ways. All over the world children love to play. The games may be different, but everyone likes having fun.

All over the world families love
their children and look after them.

All over the world children cry
when they are unhappy.

And all over the world, people worship God.

The world is full of wonderful people,
Each one unique, yet so much alike,
Sometimes happy, sometimes sad,
Curious, asking why, trying to understand.
Loving each other, needing to belong.

Welcoming new family members,
Learning to say good-bye when the time comes.
The world is full of wonderful people.
God knows each one by name.
And God loves each one.

The World is Full of Wonderful Work

People all over the world are workers. They build and they create. They grow food and they cook the food they grow. They are inventors and teachers. They are bus drivers and street cleaners. They are parents. They make pots and pans, computers, cars, toys, pencils, shoes, and bread. So much work in the world!

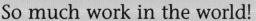

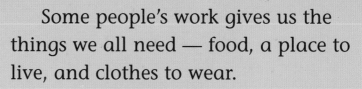

Some people's work gives us the things we all need — food, a place to live, and clothes to wear.

Some people work helps people take care of the home God has given us. They build homes that use solar power, invent cleaner fuels for cars, and discover new ways to reuse the wastes we produce.

Some people's work makes us think about how interesting and beautiful the world is. They paint pictures, compose music, and write books. They create movies, they dance, and they sing.

People's work can save lives. Doctors, nurses, firefighters, police officers, and ambulance workers — they all help to keep us safe and healthy.

We depend on the work of teachers, and of sisters and priests in our communities. We need the work of secretaries, carpenters, sales people, lawyers, truck drivers, and factory workers.

The world is full of wonderful people. The world is full of wonderful work.

God gave us this world. It is our home. It is the place where we live and where we work. We need to take care of our home and make sure that our work does not harm it.

We need each other and we depend on each other's work. Everyone's work is important. It's good to work hard and to do the best job that we can. Sometimes work is difficult. Sometimes it can be boring. But it's our work, and it needs to be done.

What kind of work do you do?

Theme 5

We Learn How to Work

Shane and Beth Carson have just turned nine. They had a family birthday party that was lots of fun. One of their cousins gave them each a model. Shane got an airplane and Beth got a car.

The twins wanted to make their models right away. But their father said they should wait. "You'll need some time," he said. "You've never made a model before."

They decided to work on the models on Sunday afternoon. Their mom and Pamela said they would help. Dad said he would help by taking Donna out.

"There are so many parts," Beth exclaimed as she emptied her box.

"Hey, look! Decals! I wonder where they go," Shane said.

"They don't go on until the very end," Pamela said.

"Do the wheels go here?" Beth asked, pointing to the axle.

"Yes, but not yet," her mother answered.

Shane and Beth began putting their models together. It was hard work because their fingers got sticky with glue. Both of them made some mistakes and had to take some pieces apart. Then they had to put them back together the right way.

"Now can I put the decals on?" Shane asked.

"No, you have to let the glue dry," his mom explained. Then she noticed what Beth was doing. "Beth! Stop putting glue on your brother's shirt!"

"But I'm bored," Beth complained. "I want to paint my car."

Their mother looked at them. "Listen," she said. "You see that coffee table? What would have happened if the person who made it was in a big hurry like you two?"

"It wouldn't look very nice?" Beth said.

"Right. And it would probably fall apart," their mom said. "It takes time to do good work. And you want to be proud of your work."

"But I want my model to be finished," Shane said.

"Me too," Beth added.

"You need to be patient," their mom said. "The first time you try something is always the hardest."

Beth and Shane had a snack while they were waiting for the glue to dry. Then it was time for painting. Shane wanted to put his decals on right away, but guess what? He had to wait for the paint to dry!

Finally, the models were done. Mr. Carson came home with Donna and he was very impressed. "You did a lot of work," he said. "Was it hard?"

"Yeah, sort of," Beth said.

Shane hung his airplane from the ceiling of his room. Beth knew that cars don't fly, but she liked the way Shane's model looked. So she hung hers from the ceiling too.

We are the work of God's hands.
The work of our hands gives glory to God.